DEMOCRACY IN POLITICS AND ECONOMICS

BY CHARLES P. TAFT

PUBLISHED FOR THE RICE INSTITUTE BY

FARRAR, STRAUS AND COMPANY

NEW YORK

Copyright 1950 by Farrar, Straus and Company. All rights reserved, including the rights to reproduce this book, or portions thereof, in any form. Manufactured in the U.S.A. by BELGRAVE PRESS, BRATTLEBORO, VERMONT.
Designed by Stefan Salter

DEMOCRACY IN POLITICS
AND ECONOMICS

Also by Charles P. Taft

WHY I AM FOR THE CHURCH

Introduction

These lectures were delivered at the Rice Institute, Houston, Texas, in April, 1949, through the generosity of Mr. James W. Rockwell who, for a number of years, has provided a series of lectures in honor of his father.

The lectures were prepared in the middle of a busy life and I am afraid that they are somewhat colloquial. They do represent, however, a philosophy that has been hammered out of a layman's experience in seeking sound ethical principles for application in the decisions and difficulties of a world that has always been tough, but today is a bit more so.

DEMOCRACY IN POLITICS
AND ECONOMICS

I

"When *I* use a word," Humpty-Dumpty said, in rather a scornful tone, "it means just what I choose it to mean—neither more nor less."

"The question is," said Alice, "whether you *can* make words mean so many different things."

"The question is," said Humpty-Dumpty, "which is to be master, that's all."

It is very easy to lose your temper when the Russians behave like Humpty-Dumpty and call their police state a true democracy, but it serves a useful purpose if it makes us stop and think what our democracy is and means to us. We are richer because the charge of "Communist!" forced David Lilienthal to burst out with his definition of democracy. We are far richer because George Marshall, from Moscow, told the world what democracy means to Americans.

We are down-to-earth people. True, we like Fourth of July oratory and we cheer for the Declaration of Independence, but in the long run we act on experience and its lessons, guided unconsciously by some deep-seated convictions about the values of Christian ideals. The strengthening of our democracy and its promotion around the world will come faster if we know more about the sources of our democratic system, and when we know more about how it actually works most effectively today. We are so likely to use tag phrases that mean little, when we ought to be analyzing what it is in our present way of living that we really cherish.* Solid history of our past and real facts of our present are the only true foundation for our ideals in this world of conflict, whether suicidal conflict with a modern Humpty-Dumpty, or conflict among pressure groups which threatens to destroy community and coöperation at home.

The history of our democracy has many roots. I am not a professional historian, philosopher, or theologian; I think, mostly, when I am driven by the requirements and the deadline for lectures and addresses. Like most laymen I can give you only a synthesis of what I read as I run.† But then what good is the professional study of history, philosophy, or theology unless its results eventually lodge in the minds of those laymen who do run as they read? So I look for the roots that help me the most, and especially the roots in religious ideals.

I begin with the very practical tradition of the English Common Law, the gradual establishment of law by com-

---

* See stimulating articles in New York *Times Sunday Magazine* by D. W. Brogan, "A Plea to America Not to Undersell Itself," November 14, 1948; by Henry Steele Commager, "Analysis of the American Character," January 2, 1949; by Storm Jameson, "Why I Can't Write About America," March 27, 1949.

† Credit largely, therefore, the authors cited in footnotes for the ideas; I am responsible for the arrangement and interpretation, and for some conclusions.

monsense decisions of the king's judge as arbitrator of each individual case as it came along, in the light of all that preceded it. I am not thinking so much of the cases I studied at law school, from which principles could be drawn, as of the continuous process which was a medieval English principle. Bracton wrote about 1250 A.D. that "Right is derived from what is unwritten and that which usage has approved." The tradition which the king as judge interpreted and declared to be custom, with the advice of his wise men in council, expanded itself gradually into the idea of a growing body of law expressing the will of the whole community. Though no writ can run against the king, said Bracton, he is subject to God and the law. The theory called clearly for the coöperation of all classes under that rule of law. Backed by that theory, the Middle Ages in England had already developed the beginnings of representative institutions that, more fully grown, could resist absolutism in England at least four hundred years later.

Fortescue three centuries after Bracton recognized especially the emphasis on economics and property in this community law. The King must stay solvent, said he, or he destroys his nation, as did many European monarchs in those very days. Fortescue appealed to the propertied men to gather in a King's Council to strengthen the economic base of the community. He was proposing no oligarchy, but a representative community interest, in distinction to the "regal" government, or despotism, which he saw all around and abhorred. Hear this, in 1546: Political government which fulfills justice and the Law of Nature can "neither make any alteration or change in the laws of the realm without the consent of the subject, nor burden them against their wills with strange impositions, so that a people governed by such laws as are made by their own consent and approbation . . . enjoy their properties securely and without the hazard of being deprived of them either by the king or by any other."*

You may wonder at such a reference to property in a discussion of the sources of democracy. We are told constantly by some today that human rights must be preferred to property rights. Fortescue would certainly have asked how you could protect human rights without protecting, as the common law did substantially, property rights of the very least of his fellow men. They were protected, even if he did not mean by the "consent of the subject" required for a change in the laws, the consent of any but property holders; and even if the penalties on the poor and the petty criminal were pretty barbarous. The law of property was protecting cherished rights among all classes.

So there is my first historical basis for our democracy, in the medieval commonsense coöperation of all classes under the rule of law, interpreted by the king for the protection of property and derived from a consent of his subjects.

A second basis is certainly in the triumph of science by the work of Galileo and Copernicus and Newton. The influence of the magician or medicine man, and the divine right of that two-forked human called a king, both began to look foolish. The common man behind the arquebus or musket destroyed the knight in armor on a great horse.

---

*Bowle, *Western Political Thought* (Oxford, 1948), 215, 224.

Science was at the beginning, and should always be, the handmaid of democratic progress. Its influence, pervasive in all our thinking, needs no defense from me. But I must point out, from Lord Lindsay, how Hobbes and Ricardo and Marx in trying to apply the rules of science to politics and social theory, thought all men alike, differing only because of environment, and subject to smart management of politician, educator, or planner.* For all the influence toward democracy of true science, Hobbes saw well enough that the only way for his kind of men to live together was by the compulsion of an omnipotent state to control the great mob of animal-like people. Even the more humane Hegel thought of the divinely constituted Leader who alone could really know what was good for the masses. The transition is direct to the "scientific" business management where there are only managers and managed. Mass propaganda is to make men even more alike—and manageable. That is a far cry from the individuals who seek willingly to coöperate in a Christian community of differing contributions to the common good.

After these two there are other roots, but I am now discussing the religious roots of democracy, or rather the specifically Christian roots, because I believe them to be the roots distinctively American. These three characteristic sources of our political tradition, Anglo-Saxon coöperation under law, the leveling of scientific discovery, and Christian inspiration, are of course not like three streams flowing separately into the river of American growth and spired our later development, quoted Bracton and Fortes-

---

*A. D. Lindsay, *Essentials of Democracy* (Oxford, 2nd ed., 1935), 1.

cue to their own uses, and were consciously or unconsciously affected by the growth of the modern scientific spirit around them. Each influence reacted upon the other, and made one stream, not several.

In speaking of the religious inspiration of democracy, as I have just indicated, I am referring to the Puritan Revolution and particularly to a certain few who took part in it. The year 1947 was the three hundredth anniversary year of a climax of that upsurge of popular ideas in England.

On October 28 and 29 and November 1, 1647, there took place in the Council of Cromwell's Army at Putney on the Thames outside London, a famous debate which is a symbol of all that inheritance. In that debate were stated many of the ideas, and even the forms of expression, that were moulded by John Locke forty years later, and became immortal in our own Declaration of Independence. It is worth knowing more about the men who coined those ideas in that debate.

Don't let the word "Puritan" deceive you into thinking of Rollin Kirby's gaunt cartoon prohibitionist with black gloves and an umbrella. The Puritans of the Revolution of three hundred years ago in England, like their contemporaries on this side of the Atlantic in that godly state, the Massachusetts Bay colony, were straight-laced and somber; but the Blue Laws were less important than the fire of their belief in the power of God working in ordinary men. That fire is what ultimately made us free, and directly inspired the words of the Declaration in 1776.

For the words "Puritan Revolution" think rather of officers and men in a New Model Army, put together in the midst of a struggle to the death between Parliament and Cavalier King Charles I. Dress them in your imagination in the great hats with flowing feathers, the long capes and great boots of those far-off times, made familiar today by long-nosed Cyrano de Bergerac on our modern stage. They were very different in temperament and beliefs, but they looked like him.

They were not wealthy, though most of the leaders, like Cromwell himself, were of good family; but they were free landholders and freeholders' sons, engaged in the quarrel as a matter of conscience. They were chosen men of good repute among their neighbors, steady, earnest, God-fearing men. One of Cromwell's enemies called them proud, self-conceited, hot-headed religious fanatics; "by their very heat and activity they bore down the rest and carried them along; these were the soul of the Army though they did not number one to twenty in it."*

Perhaps, but they gave the iron and resolution needed in a revolutionary crisis. They came, many of the men and officers too, from the small, independent religious denominations, Anabaptists, Brownists, Quakers, Separatists, and especially many calling themselves Levelers. These little sects, or "sectaries" as their fellows called them, continued to spring up in England in those post-Reformation days. The Pilgrims of Leyden were of the same group. These were indeed factious and stubborn, but they were nevertheless, as Baxter said, the very core of the Revolution and an important part of the whole Puritan movement.

---

*For this period see Morley, *Oliver Cromwell* (London, 1923); Buchan, *Oliver Cromwell* (Boston, 1934).

It was this group which made one of the three important political parties of the time. They were strongest in the army and chose their own representatives to speak for them, two from each troop, who were appropriately enough called Agitators. In addition to insisting on their pay before they disbanded, they came up with political proposals so radical that they scared the conservatives to death. They asserted the supremacy of the people instead of King or Parliament, and looked for a new governmental setup based on liberty and justice. Here was one of the controlling political elements, after the Cavaliers of King Charles had been driven away.

The Presbyterians were a second political group, not strong in the army after the fighting stopped and the chaplains went home, but with their chief support among some of the upperclass gentry backing Parliament rather than the King, and among the wealthy merchants of London. The Presbyterians had a majority of the Parliament. They wanted a church controlled by the state, retaining the King as an essential symbol of continuity, and they wanted no revolution. They proposed to suppress every other kind of religious teaching and worship. Toleration was "the Devil's Masterpiece," and to "let men serve God according to the persuasion of their own conscience" was "to cast out one devil that seven worse might enter."*

The Independents were the third political party, the middle group, led by Cromwell and by Henry Ireton, his right-hand counselor, and recently become his son-in-law. The Independents were forced gradually to oppose the

---
*Buchan, 183.

Presbyterians, but they held back from the extreme positions of the left-wingers.

In this New Model Army, besides the standing Council of War, of the higher officers only, was a General Council of the Army formed in June, 1647. Here developed the politics of the Army. There were some generals, and then from each regiment two soldiers or Agents chosen by the men, and two officers. The Agitators, not necessarily members of the Council, had prepared in consultation with their troops a proposed Agreement of the People, and had circulated it to the Army. It laid out their ideas for the constitution of the new national government.

Before this Council of the Army, the Agreement of the People was debated on this October 28, 1647, and the days following, at Ireton's headquarters, near what is now the south end of the Putney Bridge in London across from Fulham. We know what happened in a way not given by the accounts of most historical events of even more recent times, because Clarke, Secretary of the Army, took it in shorthand.*

Much of the debate centered on Proposition I of the Agreement. It read as follows:

1. That the people of England, being at this day very unequally distributed by counties, cities, and boroughs, for the election of their deputies in Parliament, ought to be more indifferently proportioned, according to the number of inhabitants.

---

* The Debates are fully set forth in Woodhouse, *Puritanism and Liberty* (London, 1938).

Every large city in the country knows what that means today, and each in its own state is fighting for reapportionment.

> Ireton interrupted the debate at once. "The meaning is that every man that is an inhabitant is to be equally considered and to have an equal voice in the election of those representatives; and if that be the meaning, then I have something to say against it."
>
> Said Colonel Rainborough of the Levelers; "I think that the poorest he that is in England hath a life to live, as the greatest he; and, therefore, truly, sir, I think it's clear that every man that is to live under a government ought first by his own consent to put himself under that government."
>
> Ireton almost sputtered as he replied: "No man hath a right to an interest or a share in the disposing of the affairs of the kingdom, and in determining or choosing those that shall determine what laws we shall be ruled by here—no person hath a right to this, that hath not a permanent fixed interest in this kingdom . . . that is, the persons in whom all land lies, and those in corporations [i.e., municipalities] in whom all trading lies. . . . By the same right of nature [by which you claim every man can vote] he hath the same equal right in any goods he sees—meat, drink, clothes—to take and use them for his sustenance. He hath a freedom to the land, to take the ground, to exercise it, till it. . . . I would fain have any man show me their bounds, where you will end, and why you should not take away all property."
>
> Rainborough: "To say because a man pleads that every man hath a voice by right of nature, that therefore it de-

stroys by the same argument all property—this is to forget the Law of God. That there's a property, the Law of God says it; else why hath God made that law, 'Thou shalt not steal'? . . . I wish you would not make the world believe that we are for anarchy."

A past president of the Federal Council of Churches could almost repeat that plea to those who shout "Communist" because one speaks in favor of dealing with human beings as children of God, equal in His sight.

Ireton could not defend against the Levelers' attack upon those "rotten boroughs" of the day, or upon the other inequities of representation, and he shifted his ground. He agreed that all seats should be equally distributed among those who rightly had a voice, without distinction. But: "If you admit any man that hath a breath and being . . . this will destroy property. . . . You may have such men chosen, or at least the major part of them, as have no local and permanent interest. Why may not those men vote against all property?" The argument against equality is ageless.

And Rainborough's brief answer is equally ageless. "I desire to know how this comes to be a property in some men and not in others."

Wildman, another Leveler, then went on to repeat the "undeniable maxim of government; that all government is in the free consent of the people." Ireton admitted the maxim, but "by the people is meant those that are possessed of the permanent interest in the land. If a foreigner comes within this kingdom . . . he, as a man, it's true, hath air, the passage of highways, the protection of laws and all that by nature. . . . But if that man be received as a being among us, I think the man may very well be content to submit himself to the law of the land; that is the law that is made by those people that have a property, a fixed property in the land. . . . Though neither he nor his ancestors did ever give concurrence to this constitution, I think this man ought to be subject to those laws . . . and so the same reason doth extend . . . to that man that hath no permanent interest in the kingdom."

"But," said Rainborough, "what hath the soldier fought for all this while? He hath fought to enslave himself, to give power to men of riches, men of estates, to make him a perpetual slave. . . . When these gentlemen fall out among themselves, they shall press the poor scrubs to come and kill one another for them."

"No," said Ireton, "the danger that we stood in was that one man's will must be a law. They thought it was better to be concluded by the common consent of those that were fixed men and settled men, that had the interest of the kingdom in them. . . . And from that way, said they, I shall know a law and have a certainty." Could one imagine an exchange more relevant to our modern problem of democracy?

These revolutionists (for they were all that, on both sides of the argument) discussed also the right of revolution. Wildman held out as a dangerous principle acting among them, the thought "that we are bound so absolutely to personal obedience to any magistrates" or "to the laws that [Parliament] shall make, though they make an unjust law," that "if they work to our destruction we may not oppose them."

Ireton's answer was that of the responsible administrator, not unlike that of Governor Hutchinson to Sam Adams in 1776: "For a man to infer that upon any particular issue you may dispute that authority . . . is commanded, whether it is just or unjust, this would be the end of all government."

So there you have in language of a distant day, but in many ways familiar, the solid arguments about the consent of the governed and equality which are the essence of the Declaration of Independence. In principle we, as Christians, are with the Levelers, though Ireton's practical arguments shake us often. Men *are* equal in the sight of God, with unassailable native rights. Certainly their property gives no sound basis for distinction. The people are sovereign, not the King, or Parliament, or the Army. They come under a government by consent or compact. Each man should vote, and in regular elections, with proper apportionment. And that they have the right of alteration or abolishment of a government destructive of these ends appears from the Leveler appropriately named Wildman.

In the one hundred and thirty years to the Declaration, things had not changed so much. Ireton's views still prevailed; the "equality" of the Declaration looked a little foolish to some, when they realized that only one in twenty-five could vote in 1789; in all but one colony there were requirements of some kind of property-holding before you could vote, following Ireton's ideas. And the spirit of the Declaration is not altogether consistent with the clear purpose of the Constitution to provide checks against the hasty, arbitrary, and perhaps tyrannical will of the majority of the people.

Even today there is a small group of tough-minded conservatives who claim we are no democracy, but a republic, and that any departure from the one to the other is a step toward our destruction. Do we really mean what our ancestors said at Putney and in the Declaration of Independence?

We had better know what we think about that, if we are to debate for men's souls along the border of the iron curtain, or to penetrate it at all. Against the fanatical possessors of all truth, we cannot put forward an equally fanatical absolutism, but we can know the grounds of our faith and our convictions. We can think out the essentials of what we believe.

So let us take a look at the Declaration of Independence itself in the light of this history and see what it actually says, and what it truly means.

"We hold these truths to be self-evident: that all men are created equal, that they are endowed by their Creator with certain unalienable rights, that among these are life, liberty and the pursuit of happiness—that to secure these rights, governments are instituted among men, deriving their just powers from the consent of the government—that whenever any form of government becomes destructive of these ends, it is the right of the people to alter or abolish it."

It is the fashion to belittle the Declaration of Independence today, either as a philosophy formulated more or less consciously by revolutionists to make themselves the chosen people for what they did, though criminals by law at the time; or as just the philosophical froth on top of the experiences and environment which are claimed as the true source of American democracy; or perhaps as just the propaganda of the ruling classes to protect their special interests. The best short answer to these cynics, learned as some are, is what Lincoln said, "I have never had a feeling, politically, that did not spring from the sentiments embodied in the Declaration of Independence."

What were the essential sentiments to which Lincoln refers? The words themselves were simple, compact, profound. They embodied a complete political philosophy. Let Lincoln himself interpret them:

> I think the authors of that notable instrument intended to include *all* men, but they did not intend to declare all men equal *in all respects*. They did not mean to say that all were equal in color, size, intellect, moral developments, or social capacity. They defined with tolerable distinctness in what respects they did consider all men created equal,—equal with 'certain unalienable rights, among which are life, liberty, and the pursuit of happiness.' This they said, and this they meant. They did not mean to assert the obvious untruth that all were then actually enjoying that equality, nor yet that they were about to confer it immediately upon them. In fact, they had no power to confer such a boon. They meant simply to declare the right, so that the enforcement of it might follow as fast as circumstances should permit.
>
> They meant to set up a standard maxim for free society, which should be familiar to all, and revered by all; constantly looked to, constantly labored for, and even though never perfectly attained, constantly approximated,

and thereby constantly spreading and deepening its influence and augmenting the happiness and value of all life to all people of all colors everywhere. The assertion that "all men are created equal" was of no practical use in effecting our separation from Great Britain; and it was placed in the Declaration not for that, but for future use. Its authors meant it to be—as, thank God, it is now proving itself—a stumbling block to all those who in after times might seek to turn a free people back into the hateful paths of depotism.*

Where did these sentiments come from—unalienable rights, equality, government by consent, the rights of revolution against destructive government? Jefferson was a broad student of all that went on in his intellectual times, and it is foolish to seek a direct source; in his mind the words grew from the whole spirit of the age. But when you go back of Jefferson and Rousseau to John Locke you arrive at two sources, Newton and the science that blasted the divine right of kings, and the Puritan revolution of 1641 to 1649, with its spiritual foundations.

While the Declaration of Independence expressed an official piety in its references to nature's God, the Creator and the Supreme Judge of the World, the philosophy of the Levelers had a less formal, yet deeper, religious foundation, and one that will not be found in the deists of the Revolution. One of the great doctrines of the Protestant reformers, derived from the prophets, was the priesthood of all believers, which meant that each person had a direct approach to God, without intervention of priest or

---

*Perry, *Puritanism and Democracy* (New York, 1944), 143.

saint or church. The Quakers called the experience the Inner Light; and from those Levelers of 1647 and from Cromwell, too, and his supporters in the great debate, came the assumption that underlay the whole discussion, namely that each person was seeking to express God's will for the group and for himself. The knowledge of that will was of course acquired through that direct communion of each with God, which each felt was his most precious inheritance.

This reliance on the inner light can be overdone. The early part of that famous debate was on the question whether the Army was bound by the prior declarations of its aims and objectives. The Levelers, with a new revelation from God, were in no temper to be stopped by an earlier party platform. As put picturesquely by a trooper, known only as Buffcoat, from the color of his uniform, "Whatsoever hopes or obligations I should be bound unto, if afterwards God should reveal himself, I would break it speedily, if it were an hundred a day." But without reliance on agreements made fairly with full knowledge, society falls apart, as Ireton argued with heated conviction.

So also the inference from the Levelers' argument is that every man must continuously consent to each act of government. But if every election must be unanimous and each person reviews the validity and application of each law, and of each administrative action, there is anarchy indeed; there is no society, no government, no action, until the impatient strong man, the Hitler, seizes power and produces action indeed.

The inner light could also be the inspiration of the intolerant religionist, whether Catholic or Calvinist, permitting no dissent, no liberty of conscience whatever. Can this fanatical belief in the voice of God in one's conscience really be a source of our democracy, or of any unity at all?

At one point in the debate in 1647 this question came into the full light of discussion. Lieutenant Colonel William Goffe, who could always be counted on for high religious concerns, criticized Cromwell because he had questioned the godly source of some prior argument: "Truly I am very tender on this thing; if we shall wait for God, and if God shall speak to us and we not hearken, we shall bring much evil upon ourselves."

Cromwell agreed that "it is a high duty" to wait upon God and listen to his voice speaking in any of us, "but when anything is spoken as from God, I think the rule is, Let the rest judge! It is left to me to judge for my own satisfaction, and the satisfaction of others, whether it be of the Lord or not, and I do no more. I do not judge conclusively, negatively, that it was not of the Lord, but I do desire to submit it to all of your judgments, whether it was of the Lord or no . . . no man receives anything in the name of the Lord further than to the light of his conscience appears."

This is an authentic note. Here is the suggestion not only of a true and free discussion, but of one resulting in a majority decision. Ireton paid lip service to the idea, but in Cromwell's mouth it comes from a deeply troubled soul truly seeking light, admitting compromise not as a concession of principle but as a recognition of fallibility. "Truly we have heard many speaking to us; and I cannot but think that in most that have spoke there hath been something of God laid forth to us; and yet there have been several contradictions in what hath been spoken. But certainly God is not the author of contradictions."

Listen, too, to Cromwell's urging to true discussion. He wished "that there may be a liberal and free debate had among us, that we may understand really, as before God, the bottom of our desires, and we may seek God together and see if God will give us a uniting spirit."

Again, "that they should not meet as contrary parties, but as some desirous to satisfy or convince each other."

Again, "If we may come to an honest and single debate, how may all agree in one common way for public good; if we may meet so, we shall meet with a great deal the more comfort and hopes of a good and happy issue, and understanding of the business."

Some may quickly say that is all very well, but it comes from a "damned psalm-singing old humbug, who cut off the head of his king,"* and put Ireland to the sword and torch; nothing that comes from him can be good. I won't stop to defend Cromwell; Lord Rosebery and John Morley and John Buchan have done it to my satisfaction. Those were hard days, but the fact remains that before the days of Cromwell inside England and outside England long after Cromwell, when you lost an election you paid for that mistake by the headman's axe. In England after Cromwell and the Puritans, and when our Anglo-Saxon idea of democracy has prevailed elsewhere, men have consented to the government of the majority, even it was of their op-

---
*Rosebery, *Miscellanies I* (London, 1921), 82.

ponents, and the losing minority was safe in its opposition. That surely was the beginning of our true modern democracy.

There was something else in this priesthood of all believers, this waiting to hear God's voice in your own conscience. You had to admit that God could speak through the others also, and that put upon you what those last exhortations of Cromwell's implied, the duty to listen.

That is not an easy obligation. I am in the profession of the law, and in the avocation of local politics; those are almost by definition controversial, argumentative. I constantly catch myself just waiting for the other fellow to finish that I may spout, and too often I listen only to be able to reply. There is no waiting for God's voice in that. That is not democracy.

I am more and more impressed with the common experience of a committee meeting, among open-minded people of good will, to discuss a difficult and complicated problem. Nearly always they come to an agreement, if they can agree, in terms different from those with which any one person started. If they disagree and the discussion was in the spirit described by Cromwell, yet they have limited the difference to the real bare bones of the issues between them, and the group loyally accepts the decision of the majority.

This solution of the democratic problem, this conference method, recognizes something else implicit in Cromwell's position in the great debate. The reason one listens for God's word in each other speaker is not only because it may be God's word and the obligation is religious. That duty to listen is also a symbol of the varying contribution each may make to the common good. The value of the contribution is just because it is different from mine, different from yours. Variety is not only the spice of life, but it is the strength of democracy. Cromwell was driven to more and more violence, caught as he was between the intolerance of the Presbyterians in Parliament and the anarchy of the Levelers and Diggers, and he cast aside most of the democratic ideas we have been examining. With his death the nation was ready at least for a restoration of relative quiet and normalcy.

But normalcy doesn't wear well when it turns into reaction, and the Revolution of 1688 brought bloodlessly a middle way completely in the British tradition. John Locke, who then set out to write the justification of revolution—which in that instance had none in theory but plenty in practice— found it in the consent of the people, the doctrine of Fortescue and of the Levelers, too; but Locke was the successor of Fortescue and Ireton, and not of Rainborough. He was the voice of the commonsense administrator who made the practical assumption that the business of government was not the spiritual salvation of the governed but their material well-being. Every man in society was to submit to the determination of the majority, but the great and chief end of men's uniting into commonwealths by consent, was the preservation of their property. Man had a property in his own person, owned by none but himself, and the labor of his body and the work of his hands was properly his. God gave the land to the use of the industrious and rational, not to the fancy of the quarrelsome and contentious.*

When Locke is carried to the logical extreme in the protection of great property and great inequality, one may well ask, with Rainborough, "how this comes to be a property in some men and not in others." This ultimate position may well cut across Locke's own principle that the well-being of all is the test of good government. Our religious principle of democracy is pretty well lost in the final common sense of the practical man, whether Locke or Ireton.

Yet the theories of the Levelers and their like were reinforced by experience in the continuing little congregations, a pretty completely satisfactory small democracy. That experience came to its full flower on the broad American continent, to which many of those congregations departed, in a largely agricultural civilization of small communities. It found almost a direct descendant in the Baptist and Methodist revivals at the turn of the eighteenth century. It spread into all the free associations of various secular kinds that are the characteristics of our American society, the town meeting, small enough to be like a congregation, the lodge, the civic association of neighbors or merchants, the social club and women's league and charitable organization.

After all, this shifting complexity of unofficial organization, which in a city like my own of Cincinnati produces the complaint frequently that we are overorganized, and

---

*Bowle, 362 ff.

in Houston has led to the prohibition of any appeal for funds not approved by a citizens' organization, is nevertheless one of the real characteristics of democratic society. These voluntary organizations accomplish community purposes, most of them, and in a completely decentralized fashion achieve many ends which government would otherwise need to seek from the center. The Nazis and Soviets always abolish voluntary organizations.

Let me summarize the core of ideas that we derive from the religious source of our democracy. Equality first. The great debate was on manhood suffrage, and on that they could not agree. But what is agreed between Ireton and Rainborough is as important as their disagreement. A man as a man has a life to live, his own, not one chosen or forced on him by another. Even a foreigner "hath air, the passage of highways, the protection of laws and all that." Where there had been a danger that one man's uncertain will must be a law, now every man could know what the law was. That is life, liberty, and the pursuit of happiness spelled out as any dweller behind the iron curtain can understand, if we let him know of it.

Close to equality came the idea, characteristically Anglo-Saxon and owing most to the medieval coöperation for the good of the realm, that each person has a contribution to make of some small view or understanding of God's purpose for the whole. Sometimes it takes religious faith to believe that about some people, but it's true.

Next, free and inquiring discussion among equals, seeking to satisfy and convince each other, and to secure a uniting spirit in seeking God together. That objective and characteristic of democratic operation is one which unfortunately can only be understood by experience. If it is difficult enough to get that kind of give-and-take of ideas among representatives of our modern pressure groups in our own country, to get prominent business or labor representatives to depart an iota from the party line of their social group, how can we expect to find that kind of free discussion in the new nations without experience, struggling to be born?

Majority decision with peaceful minority acceptance is the last, but a vast area of the globe has not progressed beyond the concept of death or exile when you lose an election.

So you can see why I lay so much emphasis on religion for the true democracy I cherish. Figgis is altogether right in saying, "Political liberty, as a fact in the modern world, is the result of the struggles of religious organisms to live." We may well have the conviction that only experience of the free, even fragmented, congregation which is one direct product of the Reformation, could have produced our democracy. And it must be pointed out to some who deny the origins of any democracy in Protestantism, that I am talking about Baptists and Congregationalists and Quakers, not about Lutherans or Presbyterians, or even my own Episcopalians. It was essentially the Baptist and Methodist revivals that broke down the property qualifications for voting in these United States between 1789 and 1852.

These essentially Christian ideas from Bracton and Fortescue and the Levelers and Cromwell are fundamental, but unfortunately they don't solve our modern problem. They are supremely effective in the little group, which decides its own policies and then, with some slight division of labor, carries them out through all its members.

But what if the constituency is 2,000 in a modern urban church, or 100,000 in a city, or 7,000,000 in an industrial and agricultural state like Ohio, or 150,000,000, or 2,000,000,000? There, clearly, you have to separate those who decide the policies from those who carry them out; and the larger the organization, the simpler must be the questions of policy for the whole constituency to decide.

There is where you have to face the practical questions raised by Ireton, and much later by Burke. How can you rely on the consent of the non-technical governed, for decision of complicated technical questions of today? You set up a representative system to meet the necessity of bigness, and how can you permit such a legislative operation to depend on Gallup polls, on counting the mail for and against? You must seek ways to make the representatives, the rulers *pro tem* between elections, responsible men, conscious of values, eager to apply them in reaching sound decisions in the public interest. That was Burke's great contribution.*

But I wish to go further in these discussions—into a field less understood. Everyone knows the standard arguments on this last point of representative government. Have you thought, however, about whether these democratic principles apply in administration, in the organizations—public

---
*Bowle, 430.

or private—we set up to accomplish our community and economic and social purposes, to carry out our decisions? Is there any democracy in leadership and management? Can we have both freedom and obedience? How, too, shall we have a conference process and democratic ideas in competing groups, often interrelated in complicated ways?

II

I HAVE tried to analyze the contribution historically of religious ideas to our democratic philosophy and method. The Christian ideals show up in the medieval theory of co-operation of all classes under the rule of community law, in the idea of equality, of the contribution to the community by each member of it, and in the concept of a full free discussion among men of good will seeking God's purpose. The concession to fallibility implied in acceptance of majority decision in spite of one's convictions is after all not un-Christian, for it is surely Christian doctrine that we humans can only see through a glass darkly. It is always worth while to recall Gamaliel: if the idea springs from men, it will collapse; if it springs from God, you will be unable to put it down; you may find yourself unknowingly fighting against God! There are good compromises, as well as bad.

But I also pointed out that there is not much help in direct Christian teaching about the application of those democratic ideas, so successful in a small congregation, to a city or state, to a big organization, or to the interaction of competing organizations in a single community, of the kind which are universally characteristic of our urban industrial civilization. The usual exposition of the Bible does not tell you much about the problem of the executive, or the frustration of a little man in a little group way down the line in a big organization.

Worse than that, there is very little in general education about the processes or the social skills these problems require. I am not at all sure that even the vocational training in the social sciences really makes the point. My daughter, who has been a student of social work, questioned that statement when I was discussing with her my general thesis in these lectures. It is true, as she pointed out, that there has been a lot of work done on groups, their psychology and operation, in the field we call sociology, and it has expanded into the techniques of community organization. But there is certainly something lacking in that approach. I struggled during the war with the organization of communities for better service to soldiers, and they did well, but without much help from social workers and sociologists; interested politicians and intelligent active mothers of families were far more effective. In the war-boom industrial communities we had an awful time getting any organization formed at all in which people would coöperate, not to mention taking leadership. This social-work approach somehow fails to see the whole problem; it leaves out the executive function, the problem of management and leadership in organization.

When you come to management, there are plenty of schools of business administration, and a huge literature of techniques of management. But somehow that has left out much of the human and social factor which gets too much attention in the other approach. The technique of coöperation, the social skills of dealing with people—these seem to be inadequate in all this vocational training as well as in our general education.

The churches have learned a lot about social work, nothing about management and responsible decision in the lay world, and almost nothing about the possibilities for application of religion in these coöperative processes that hold organization together. All of us live in coöperative systems, simple or complicated, all of a kind where religion is of the very essence as a lubricant, and yet we are seldom taught anything about these social skills.

Let's take a look at formal organizations as they are so skillfully dissected by Chester Barnard of the New Jersey Telephone and Rockefeller Foundation.* Their striking characteristic is how short-lived they are. Except for the Catholic Church and some universities and a few kingdoms, and a few like the Royal Society, there are almost none over two hundred years old. Our own nation is not a youngster but an oldster, practically the oldest of modern democracies. Read "Fifty Years Ago" in the daily papers and notice how many organizations are mentioned which you never heard of. Think of organizations you belonged to, and recall their struggles, often unsuccessful, for survival.

That is not by chance. It is because formal organiza-

---

* Barnard, *Functions of the Executive* (Cambridge, 1946).

tion is not easy at all, and it is also in part because we haven't studied how people coöperate, which is the heart of formal organization.

I pause to remark that I am not talking about coöperatives, which are an important form of business organization. All organizations are coöperative systems, and I am talking about skills needed universally, not just in one kind of organization.

Another characteristic of formal organizations is how alive they are. Each is new and different, and each is different, too, from the mere sum of its individuals. It is a true social creature, an entity. In the State Department during the war, I put together first a division and then an office which finally had some forty men. They were all from general business, in service for the duration, working on the wartime diplomatic problems of procurement and supply, as liaison between the War Production Board and other government agencies, and the geographical political desks in State. For a year, they grew into an identifiable unity and effectiveness. Then a reorganization absorbed them and gradually the entity disappeared. New entities took its place if the function needed doing. I suppose it is a little like Paul's word, "What you sow never comes to life unless it dies." This is part of continuous process.

This unique and identifiable character is because the organization is made up of human beings with personality, with immense power of choice, with adaptability. An organization is a field of personal forces, like a magnetic field, or rather like competing overlapping magnetic fields. Its success depends upon the willingness of the individuals to join the organization and to continue with it. The willingness fluctuates tremendously. Good Friday of 1949 brought out a crowded changing mass of people in my church, which must have totalled twenty-five hundred in the three hours in a sanctuary that holds perhaps eight hundred or nine hundred. Our annual meeting of the church Monday night had two hundred and fifty. A class of boys I used to have might reach twenty on a Sunday out of thirty on the list, or it might dwindle to five. What do we really know about what incentive, what motivation brings or keeps a person in an organization? What do we really know about our own incentives?

Organization for its success has to have purpose. Its members must have something to do, or it never gets off the ground. Though it once starts, without continuous purpose it disintegrates. The purpose has to be close and specific in the small group; for the larger, it almost has to be general, intangible, probably sentimental. The most effective is belief in a cause, rather than intellectual understanding of detailed general objectives.

That knowledge of purpose and belief in general objectives obviously requires communication effective between individuals from top to bottom of the organization. But in the ordinary case how can one person communicate effectively to more than a small group? Jack & Heintz can put in a loud speaker that reaches every corner of the plant, but there is no possibility of direct reaction in question or discussion from the "associates." There is communication between a conductor and a symphony orchestra, a minister preaching and his congregation, the President broadcasting at a moment of national emergency or international concern. But for communication in each of those expanded groups, there has been infinite prior preparation, largely by personal experience and contact. The amount a person can really give out to others has its limitation. Most groups with effective cohesion and intercommunication cannot be larger than fifteen or twenty. Group decision in executive management today is common; the Ford Company is said to have a rule that not over five or six persons shall make up any such group. Communication is not just transmission by voice or paper or wire of a word. It takes a real sharing of ideas and mutual understanding, a process that uses up the transmitter's energy and is subject to the definite physical limitations of an individual.

This is an extremely important fact which is basic in our life and often ignored in our thinking. A big organization, even in the form of a city like Houston, or the Farm Bureau, or the CIO, is not a horde of thousands or millions of people. Every one of those three is in fact made up of little interlocking groups, of about ten people on the average, tied together into work groups or families or neighborhood and other social groups. Even in the hierarchies of U.S. government employment, or of Procter and Gamble, or Monsanto Chemical, a regional director at Dallas or a plant manager at Texas City goes to Washington or St. Louis for a meeting of regional directors or plant managers where he is just one of a crowd presided over by somebody higher; at home he has a group of his top executives over which he presides. Each of that group heads up another group below (or out from the center, if you prefer that image).

The plant manager's effectiveness at work may depend on how his family group at home is functioning, or on the demands on his bank account from trying to keep up with the Joneses in the local country club, or in the lodge. Man is not a grain in a social sand heap of undifferentiated individuals moved by a shovel in the hands of the one who controls the media of mass propaganda; he is a social animal in a complex of many groups. Only the man in the study really believes in "the masses."

Much of this, so far as it is in a single organization, shows up on a chart. But behind every chart is an informal organization which in many spots on the chart makes hash of logic. You know the questions you ask when you come into a strange outfit: What is the "lowdown" around here? Who's the real boss? Where are the wreckers you have to look out for? The social groups in an organization, which may or may not parallel the chart, are extremely important to the effective working of the whole, and you have to look to find them.

Surely every businessman has had the experience of looking at a lop-sided chart, and on inquiry finding that it is that way because of the particular abilities or quirks of particular individuals. On the chart of the United States Government you don't find anything about national party organizations, but they affect the operation, you may be sure. On the chart of the Democratic Party across the nation, you don't see anything about Dixiecrats, or conservative Republicans . . . but!

An important factor in the existence of the informal organization is that it is an outlet through which a person can exercise independent choices, not tied down by the limitations of the formal organization. One can be sure that there are associations like that in Russia, where no formal organization can exist not dominated by the Communist Party (except perhaps the Orthodox Church, and the independent churches). Informal organizations like that help to give that sense of individual integrity and significance, of self-respect which a person who is lost in a big formal organization must find, or rebel. If the management can't or won't give it to him, he turns inevitably to "informal organization," or to another formal organization like a union, to find it.

The structure and cohesion of all these little interlocking groups in our society of formal organizations is certainly built on the individual instincts, habits, and desires of their members. What makes them do what they do, or not do when they balk? I do not wish to enter into a long discussion of motivation and incentives and how they can be changed by coercion or persuasion, but I must make a few more points.

The most important fact which we moderns have almost lost sight of is best summed up in the philosophy of Quesnay, who wrote as one of the principal French physiocrats about 1750. He was a doctor, a clinician at the court of Louis XV. He claimed that there is a natural and essential order of society in which, if a number of individuals work together to achieve a common purpose, a harmony of interest will develop among them to which each will willingly subordinate his self-interest. That is profoundly true and is a principle to which religion and the churches should have clung as basic for a true society.

Instead, many of us have unconsciously accepted the completely materialist teaching of David Ricardo and Karl Marx at the same time that we damn materialism and shudder at Communism.

Ricardo was a London stockholder who took the teachings of the humane Adam Smith and invented, from his country estate with his rich wife, that imaginary economic man who was moved solely by a logical self-interest. He dreamed up the falsehood that if an immense herd of such individuals were turned loose in a free market without any government intervention, the laws of supply and demand would automatically produce harmony and justice. It is not true, but unfortunately, while we know that today, all of us, including our leading preachers, keep thinking and saying, or complaining, that self-interest is really what makes the world go round. The extreme to which that can be carried was when my good friend, Dave Lawrence, vigorously attacked the Federal Council of Churches two years ago for a pamphlet which undertook to analyze the non-profit incentives in our economy. Lawrence claimed that was an undercover Communist attack on the "profit system." Self-interest is not what makes our system go, and Ricardo's theory of *laissez-faire* must be condemned by the churches.

Karl Marx reaches the same result by a different approach and is just as bad as (but no worse than) Ricardo. Marx says that spiritual ideals are just a fraud propagated by the ruling classes to keep their power; the only true influence on the development of cultures and civilization is the way men earn their living, the particular system of production.

Of course, material incentives are important and the current ways of producing goods and services are fundamental in their influence. But the instinct of human association in achieving a common purpose constantly leads men to yield their material incentives, including even the physical conditions of work they might prefer.

Certainly one of the important incentives is a sense of accomplishment, of performance up to one's capacity, reflected perhaps in the respect and admiration of one's fellows.

Growing in part from that, is the desire for prestige and then for power and influence, an urge to share in big events, to control one's destiny. Power is one of the dangerous motives, clearer to religious thinkers in all its phases than almost any other.

The power of ideals can be dominant, as we saw with Cromwell's Ironsides. It may be expressed in the sense of craftsmanship, the sense of tidiness that must be involved, I suppose, in spring cleaning. It may be what is usually thought of in the term ideals, liberty, justice, religion. Stalin had to draw on that when he reopened the Orthodox Churches, in the crisis of war.

But I must come back again to what is probably the greatest incentive for ordinary people, the effects of habitual and customary association with those you like in carrying out a purpose in which you agree. That somehow gives a security of a social character to replace what the industrial revolution nearly destroyed. Should anything be of greater concern to Christians than what has happened to people crammed together for machine production in cities so big that they destroyed all sense of neighborhood? But some of the very careful reports on these effects of the industrial revolution in the last century in France, for instance, were never translated from French to English, and our parish churches and congregations have gone on teaching the religion that grew up in little farming communities, without ever analyzing this basic human desire for effective association. They have completely failed to study the ways in which people can find real security right in a factory, or large insurance company, or government office. The Communists saw it, and solidarity is their term which really sums up this most powerful incentive, upon which they constantly attempt to play.

Let me give you a very interesting example. Lord Lindsay once described what happened in the labor battalions in France in the first war, where the money incentive, the cash nexus, disappeared completely and the general motive was assumed to be patriotic.* An army or division commander, or the engineers, ordered a hundred men from a labor battalion for a job, and hoarded them when it was done because he didn't know whether he could get them the next time in competition with other demands. Was hoarding labor then due to the profit motive?

The men at first were picked at random from different companies, and worked under N. C. O.'s of the employing division or engineers. Their work, unless it was clearly a war emergency at the front, was slovenly and ineffective.

---

*Lindsay, *Christianity and Economics* (London, 1933), 155.

DEMOCRACY IN POLITICS AND ECONOMICS

The first step taken was to send, not miscellaneous workmen but a company, a platoon, an existing unit with an existing morale. That was much better. But the next and most important step, not always possible, unfortunately, was to require from the division commander, whom you might call the employer, the requisition, not of men, but of a job. Then the labor battalion decided how many men it took to do it, and even beyond that undertook the job under its own leadership. That changed the whole spirit of the enterprise. Though unskilled labor, there were nevertheless tricks of the trade, "know-how," which built pride and efficiency. That is what I meant by power of choice. Giving that kind of independence builds self-respect and integrity. If the employer doesn't give scope for it, the union or the Commies will.

It is equally important to realize just what is the nature of the process by which orders for a program of an organization are made effective. I remember when I was small standing in front of a mirror and saying "I am the Governor of the Philippine Islands." In my mind, you see, was the thought that as Governor, my father just had to give an order and it was done. Some people try that. That is the theory evidently of the Communist mentality, of the fourteen men in the Politburo; they establish the line for the party, not to be questioned, and they must be rather continuously irritated to find that factory managers, even bureau heads, disobey, for their own profit, or other good reason (even their incapacity or inability to perform), try to conceal their disobedience, and suffer the extreme penalties they knew they risked.

For, you see, one of the most constant characteristics of orders is that they are ignored or disobeyed. That is especially true of laws and regulations. They're all right for somebody else, but they don't mean me. What's the Constitution among friends? Watch a long procession of cars in moving traffic going at a steady forty miles past signs that say "Speed Limit 35 m.p.h." Even the great bulk of our obedience is in the zone of indifference, where it is either less trouble to obey than not to obey, or where we obey just out of general loyalty to the organization, but without enthusiasm.

These remarks may prepare you a little for Chester Barnard's definition of authority, which at first seems revolutionary, but which on the contrary makes complete sense, and which begins to give some glimmer of how democracy works: Authority is the willingness and capacity of men to submit to the necessities of coöperative systems. Not the power of Napoleon or Hitler or Stalin or Khan, but the acceptance of all the executives and officers and supervisors and little people. The organization which is successful is the one where the acceptance is eager and interested; the failure is likely to be the one where the order and program meets indifference and resistance.

Some people will say that is a platform of chaos, a giving up of the rights of management. But you certainly know that no competent executive gives an order that he knows can not or will not be obeyed. The inexperienced operator does just that as proof of his incapacity, and the organization disintegrates.

The order has to be understood, which means clear-channel interpretation and communication. The man receiving it, the more important and effective a cog he is, must believe it not inconsistent with the general purpose of the organization (even in the Army); he must see it as part of a social process that gives him personal incentive; and he must be physically and mentally capable of doing it.

But the process is more than those simple rules of Mr. Barnard. The flesh on those bare bones is the conference process. Take D-Day, June 5, 1944. In the ground forces, air forces, and naval operations of the United States and the United Kingdom there were innumerable written orders and as much verbal direction. Suppose by a miracle (for it would take that) those orders were all worked out by Eisenhower's top staff of a dozen men, and handed out on June 1, 1944. Could the operation have been started on June 5, stopped, and completed on June 6? The answer is, clearly, No; but it is worth analyzing why. The reason the assumption is impossible and the operation would not work is that those orders were not the product of one brain, Eisenhower's, or of his twelve top men; they were the result of an infinite number of conferences and practice operations, from which came changes in the orders, made partly by the top men but to a surprising degree, I am certain, by contribution and suggestion by subordinates. On June 6, 1944, it is safe to say that from half to three-quarters of the men and women involved and perhaps even more did their jobs better, followed their instructions more eagerly, because they had each participated in preparing the instructions, shared in the development of the program, had had an opportunity of independent choice and decision in some small degree.

The manager will say: "That was war time; sure, everybody worked together; this is peace. I agree all right with the necessity for good communication well interpreted; and only a dumbbell would give a man an order he can't carry out. But this business of the fellow under me telling me it isn't what the company wants, or he isn't interested anyway; by God, I'm telling him what the company wants, and he'd better do it, or else!"

Yes, compulsion can change incentives, but the best smart foremen don't do it that way. They persuade, rationalize, appeal to a company or unit patriotism. They want eager and interested acceptance, not grudging obedience. They will try to turn a man's motivation to help them, not hinder.

What if the argument is on some phase of the company's business that the manager feels is none of the employees' business, pricing policies or output schedule? That is not likely to happen in the case of an individual employee, but it does or can in a bargaining session. Is that an interference with the rights of management? Chamberlain at Yale has done a very interesting book on that subject which is worth summarizing briefly.* Labor-management relationships on the *execution* of plans and production ought not to be difficult. Execution does not involve much discretion, and determining whether something was done as it was

---

*Chamberlain, *The Union Challenge to Management Control* (New York, 1948).

supposed to be done is a relatively simple question of fact.

But decisions on policy, and decisions on the methods by which policy is to be carried out, are the place where unions want to participate, and management doesn't want them. That conflict needs to be analyzed, however. Policy on what? Chamberlain breaks down decisions on policy into eight or ten general fields, with further subheads under each.

In the field of personnel is the deepest and broadest union participation, in hiring and firing, in discipline, in wages and hours, in promotions and seniority and vacations and health provisions, in type of personnel and its allocation.

Procurement and finance problems stir little interest in union leaders; so, also, for cabinet or staff functions like key personnel selection, research, public and trade and industry relations. But a characteristic of the development of these relationships is that within a general field, of the kinds I have just been mentioning, if the union gets participation in one element it is likely to move on to others in the same field. In production, unions are chiefly concerned with job content, methods and standards that affect rates, machinery that reduces immediate jobs. Do they then move into the area of design and engineering? They have in the needle trades. In distribution they would seem to have little interest, until a secondary boycott on an outlet pops up, or until the pressure for security in a seasonal industry creates a demand for an annual wage and requires discussion of distribution.

These are all practical questions. If the employees on the

committee, or the union representatives, are competent in the particular field (and good management can handle them if they're not), why can't they make a real contribution in the conference process and give us a better decision by management in the end?

Well, the manager had something when he said that Eisenhower was successful because it was war time. Everyone agreed on the objectives and purposes of the operation and of the war. But are the objectives of the company and the union the same? They frequently are not. How, then, can you get a decision by agreement, instead of violent disagreement and an impasse? If that kind of opposition exists, you can see why the employer will not give in. If that kind of union wants a closed shop, you can see why the employer will fight till hell freezes over.

Note that this is not a question of any majority decision of employees; nobody proposes that; it is a question of the success of the conference process from top to bottom. Harry Bridges says frankly in the Communist tradition that the interests of employers and employees are diametrically opposed and that they can never coöperate. John L. Lewis does not say it that way, but the history of his negotiations over the years shows that with all the tremendous advance from what used to be shocking conditions, he has always denied any interest or concern in the economic success of the employer who makes his jobs. Walter Reuther, an old-line Socialist, finds it difficult to get away from the tradition of the class struggle. Some of that is the product of internal union politics, but the contrast with Hillman and Dubinsky in the needle trades and Rieve in the Textile Workers is very great. These latter truly work with employers once an agreement is reached, and have even advanced loans or bought stock in order to keep a plant going where their men are employed.

This question of coöperation or war is far more than a union-management battle. When labor gets political power in Britain, and Government takes over certain industries, or when people build up a great coöperative store or a mutual insurance company, there still are managers and employees, and our coöperative systems can only work in any field if we seek coöperation. They can work best if we seek it in Cromwell's injunction to seek a unifying spirit under God. The churches need to learn and study how all these organizations work, but once they have a basis of knowledge they must go back to the principle of coöperation of all classes for the good of the community which they worked out in the Middle Ages, and they must demand that kind of coöperation today. In each organization there has to be, from the intelligent effort of every element, agreement on common objectives and an effective development of incentives that contribute to it.

Unions and management meet within a single organization, but they also meet as separate competing organizations. That may be before a Senate Committee on Labor and Public Welfare, or it may be when they are brought together by a church organization in an effort to perform its ministry of reconciliation. The church, on the other hand, may find management problems within its own organization, in the form of influential members and financial supporters of a congregation; or it may meet labor or agriculture as a group to whom it has not adequately extended, but should extend, its ministry by promoting rural work, organizing a working class parish, or establishing an industrial chaplaincy. The church may even find itself as employer dealing with a union whose objectives are far from its own, as when Church World Service in its West Coast warehouses has to contract with Harry Bridges' longshoremen.

The difficulty in all those situations is just like what I have described within an industrial organization—how do you achieve the conference process when a person is bound down to his party line and can concede nothing because he is not an individual, but a spokesman for a group? The answer is that you don't, until you get some little of both Buffcoat's determination to speak only his own conscience, and Cromwell's unity in seeking God. Do we want unity, or do we want war? Do we approach other people in the spirit quite wrongly attributed to Paul, "Come out from among those of ungodly beliefs: how can light associate with darkness?" Or do we work and pray as did Jesus, that we may all be one?

Mary Follett had the right idea of it:* What we want is not power *over*; it is power *with*. Control should mean not the edict of a Hitler, but fact-control as the controller of a company keeps up with the facts of a company; plus coördination and correlation in the kind of process which I have described as the conference process. Our alternatives are not unrestricted liberty on one side and executive or government coercion on the other. Coördination means a

---
*Follett, *Dynamic Administration* (New York, 1942).

self-control or self-regulation in the interest of the common objectives, of the community good.

Here are Miss Follett's four principles of coördination between organizations:

First is cross-relations between heads of different departments, between spokesmen of different interests, between operating people of different groups, all at corresponding levels—not a channel all the way up to the President and across to the other President and down to the working representative of the other crowd.

Next, is to insure that those contacts are made early before ideas have hardened.

Next, is to insure that the contacts are made between every element that is concerned. A discussion in the State Department on surplus property disposal of aviation equipment on French airfields had to bring in French economic, French political, finance, surplus, and aviation divisions. That interpenetration of every part by every other part is essential; it can't be done by Washington for Cincinnati; only by the parts where they are, and by voluntary action.

Last and most important of Miss Follett's concepts of coördination is that if it works, it produces continuous and spontaneous change. I implied that in my description of the conference process. It is profoundly true that coördination exists to adapt organizations to change.

But that is also one of our most profound difficulties, for ordinary people don't like change. In an agricultural civilization people were stable, doing what their ancestors did; as someone remarked about agriculture in Alabama in the last generation, it was a set of inherited motions. The cotton picker and now the leaf dissolver, if they work, will upset us right down to our marrowbones. Yet that adaptation to change is exactly what we have to learn as a civilization. We have to find what are the basic values to which we owe our strength and what are the frills and husks we can discard. We have to keep relaxed and unshaken when those frills and husks we are accustomed to see and use, blow up in our faces. But we can't keep unshaken without a firm hold on the basic values.

What has our educational system, theoretical and practical, done to acquaint us with either the complexities of the organizations in which we live, or the values that can hold us straight?

III

I WISH to review my own educational experience in order to see how it prepared me either to know and appreciate the Christian values most important in our culture and democracy, or to know and understand the complexity of organization to which those values must be applied today.

My education in religious principles began with the study of the Bible in Sunday School; from that I got a general knowledge of its contents, but none of its origins and none of the depth of its thinking. Job and Jeremiah were closed books. From the age of eleven until I came back to Cincinnati after law school, my religious experience was the usual one in the school and college Christian Association: emphasis on the New Testament, on personal conversion, and especially on the Christian vocations. The relevance of religious thinking to the hard ethical problems of society was hardly suggested. I remember wondering a bit idly what was involved when someone jocularly remarked that my classmate H. Hadley was pondering the problem of evil. Philosophy, perhaps because of the teacher, was a good deal of a bore. Perhaps a college youngster wasn't mature enough; perhaps the G.I.'s since the war have found in the regular courses more than I did. The main assumption was that all choices in life were simple, black and white, like whether you should get tight, or neck a girl.

As to my educational program in school and college, there was something of the idea that certain things like Latin and mathematics trained the mind; there was some concern for a broad choice of history, language, literature, and science, and some thought that certain courses were preparatory for a legal career, like English History and English Constitutional History under George Burten Adams. From the *Trivium* of the old days I had grammar and a little rhetoric, especially in a very valuable course in Daily Themes; and logic from a fairly long study of mathematics. Astronomy I never got, or music beyond "Columbia the Gem of the Ocean" in public primary school and popular classics in the mandolin and banjo clubs at private secondary school. Not much of the *Quadrivium*!

The Harvard study of *General Education in a Free Society** tells me that I went through a process of having opened before my mind the intellectual forces that have shaped the Western mind; because I studied the past I am supposed to have confronted, in some form or other, the philosophic and religious fact of man in history and to have recognized the huge continuing influence alike on past and present of the stream of Jewish and Greek thought in Christianity. Because I knew modern democracy I knew

---
*Cambridge, 1945.

something of Jefferson; because I respected freedom of speech and the rights of private conscience I was not wholly ignorant of Milton's *Areopagitica* or Sophocles' *Antigone*.

Well, maybe, but I feel more like saying to those distinguished educators, Sez you!

Why shouldn't I be told when I am being educated what is being done to me and why? Nobody told me that the Greco-Roman tradition and the Jewish-Christian were the two great streams that made Western civilization. When I read it as Walter Lippmann had expressed it at the American Association for the Advancement of Science four or five years ago, all my past training let me see that truth and it became part of my intellectual equipment; it wasn't before that. Again the Harvard study says that a basic concept of the Western tradition is a belief in man's dignity and a recognition of his duty to his fellow men. That I recognized long since, but not from any of my formal education, however implicit it may have been. I did know that man was a child of God owing him the duty of loving him with all heart and soul and mind, and that one should love neighbor as oneself.

So when you come to the problems of human relations, nobody need expect that children and youngsters will learn social skills adequately by osmosis, through the pores of the skin. Human organization can be studied, and the tough problems of choices as well, with their moral and ethical overtones. I suppose "Social Studies" does that a little in secondary schools, but why aren't we told about the churches as social and community phenomena? That last has the highest Jewish, Catholic, and Protestant approval, but it is not often done. I didn't get it in school or college.

Law school did not give me much more of human relations as such. When I spoke at the opening of the Yale Law School building sixteen years ago, I told them they should add to the curriculum a course in dickering. Why not? Aren't there principles of negotiation that one could learn?—like never letting oneself get put in the spot where the other fellow knows you can decide a proposition all by yourself; you must always have somebody you have to go back and consult with.

Law school and even more experience in frequent trial of criminal cases in the Prosecutor's office did give me something important—great respect for facts and their clear presentation; and at the same time full realization how slippery facts are when you see them through even honest eyes that are humanly fallible.

Within a few months of my arrival in Cincinnati I was chairman of a Community Chest district that ran from downtown slums along the river seventeen miles to the next county line. Getting people to work for that was easy preparation for the human and organization problems of local politics. There was the enthusiasm of a crusade, the coöperation of devoted leaders, the extraordinary effectiveness of simple ideas, and the essential compromises that "included in" as candidates people not quite so devoted, not quite so single-minded. The long history, as reform movements go, twenty-five years now, has seen all the problems and exhibited all the principles of organization I have set out. But nobody had set them out for me in usable fashion until I found Chester Barnard and Elton Mayo.* After you play by ear for a generation it is not so easy to compose by planning the notes. It would have been much better if it had been a part of my education.

From my Community Chest relation I found myself drafted in charitable organizations. Besides some educational experience as treasurer and investment officer (something, too, for which lawyers and business men ought to be trained), I learned gradually about social work, until as chairman of the City Council Welfare Committee during the recession of 1938 I really had a baptism of fire and learned at first hand how people feel in want and unemployment, and how cruel some administrators can be who don't have a real religious foundation.

A little later, from 1940 to 1943, I built two hundred and seventy-five small houses in the lowest possible price range. I was startled to find how suspicious and totally unreasonable ordinary people could be. And yet as I thought about it, it was surely just evidence of how people in that economic group, who were buying houses for $3800 in 1940, had been imposed upon in all their dealings with people who sold them things. Their suspicion was all unnecessary, too, for besides getting good houses, they can all sell their houses now for twice what they paid or more; I lost my shirt building the first half and barely got it back on the second.

Meanwhile, having gotten into City Council and having had considerable experience in practising law, and in acting as a labor mediator for the government, I was strug-

---

*Mayo, *Social Problems of an Industrial Civilization* (Cambridge, 1945).

gling with the problem of compromise. I read F. S. Oliver's very stimulating book, *The Endless Adventure,* but when I spoke of it to church groups, my very good friend, the Y secretary, also a Methodist minister, shuddered and told me I shouldn't. Yet, as I think I demonstrated in my first lecture, political compromise instead of civil war to the death was the Anglo-Saxon invention that made democracy possible. The refusal to compromise in Mr. Gromyko's "No!"—carried over now only too often into the techniques of American pressure groups—is something that can tear us apart. It stems from modern insistence on infallibility. I was much interested to see recently a report of a speech by Sir Norman Angell, who pleaded for a sense of the fallibility of our judgment and confirmed my own opinion when he called that sense "a moral quality." Yet all my religious training had been quite on the side of the Methodist Y Secretary that black was black and white was white and "compromise" must be evil.

In City Council in Cincinnati and as a responsible officer of our fusion movement, I was faced with the question whether I should conduct a crusade to get rid of bingo, when not only the vote in Council was seven to two against me, but two of the seven for bingo were on my side in the fusion movement and were quite conscientiously not at all disturbed by bingo. To put on the fight meant to split our side right down the middle, and jeopardize the good government movement. A fine young Episcopal minister, my own assistant rector, was sure I should. I didn't. Not much help from the church there.

In fact the church hasn't given us laymen in recent

generations much help in dealing with what I prefer to call the perversity of human beings. They can denounce sin, which I suppose is the same thing; but how is one supposed to feel and act in the face of utterly unreasonable stubbornness of the politicians on the other side, or the power companies, or the labor unions, or anybody who doesn't agree with you? The other fellow is so seldom sweetly reasonable, or ready to agree on the same objectives and purposes. Look how people vote in elections. I don't mean the presidential election of 1948. I am thinking of how our Cincinnatians voted on some twelve or thirteen bond issues at the same election. From the perversity of one's opponents when they are in the driver's seat, and of the electorate too often, a person finds total frustration, and my education in religion and philosophy gave me little preparation to deal with that. I've had to dig it out myself the hard way.

The digging came in considerable part when I was teaching a church school class, not from any formal preparation the church gave me but from feeling around my own way, buying books from the book reviews both American and British (the *Times Literary Supplement* from London).

This was brought more or less to a head when John R. Mott induced me to go to the great conference on Church, Community, and State at Oxford in 1937, from which with the nearly simultaneous Edinburgh conference came the World Council of Churches.

At Oxford I learned for the first time something about theology, and I had the fascinating experience of watching theological application to the current problems of society guided by such extraordinarily able minds as Reinold Niebuhr, John Baillie, Paul Tillich, Sir John Maud, Canon Demant, and John Bennett. Much Christian dynamic had come from my great rector in my church at home, but none of that intellectual content. Preachers by and large, no matter how good pastors they are, either don't have that to give, or they keep it to themselves. That first contact with the worldwide movement for greater unity in the churches brought with it two convictions. The first is that our Christian religion is almost meaningless if it is to be confined to preaching the gospel on Sunday. If it is not a religion and a religious philosophy which can explain my daily life for me and give an integrating principle for dealing with all the social problems and perversity and plain human nastiness we have to encounter from Monday to Saturday, I am not interested in it. Someone asked me recently why the preachers kept talking about other things than religion—social welfare and raising money and so on; shouldn't they get back to religion? There are two phases to answering that. As Fortescue said in 1450, the king had to be solvent to be of any use, and so does the church. The pastor in my church is the administrator, and he has to see that the finances and administration are well handled. He ought not to do it himself, as many try to do; he ought to come trained, or be trained by his board or vestry; if he isn't, to enlist laymen and merely direct the job in their hands. The other part of the answer is that unless his preaching is in terms and parables that are related to the daily living of men today, he'd better quit preaching. Jesus' parables were just that, but we live in a different civilization from rural and commercial Palestine of 30 A.D. To get parables for today takes thinking, for it means a study of how Jesus' principles can and should apply in a completely different setting. A social gospel with no fundamental theology is no good, but theology without a social gospel is wasted breath on us laymen.

The movement for Christian unity and for application of Christian principles in politics and economics ran into some more perversity. A small but vociferous minority, with that peculiar brand of unscrupulousness which sometimes attaches to religion, has done everything in its power to undermine the great Christian denominations around the world, but especially in this country. I certainly respect sincere differences in religious opinion, whether more conservative or more radical than my own views. They make a contribution to our common thinking, as I hope I can; and as Cromwell said, "I cannot but think that in most that have spoke there hath been something of God laid forth to us." But when our objectives reach a complete divergence and all pretense of Christian charity seems abandoned, when the deeply spiritual men and women of great and varied gifts who are seeking God together are described not just as false prophets and darkness, but as leprosy and Jezebel, I can only do what Jimmy Gleason once advised in an old-time comedy, "just act like they wasn't there."

But I have learned about human relations from them, also, and if ever I have to live with them I suppose I would be ready to scrap my own advice and act as we must with the similar absolutists, the Russians. In fact all of this democracy competes in our world with the absolutist, and the competition is tough. We in the free nations must be respectful of the other fellow's ideas; we wait and see; we concede something; perhaps we even agree to a compromise. The absolutist is insistent, arbitrary, unyielding, and rapid in action. He seems to have the advantage, and psychologically he seems to be supremely confident of his everlasting infallibility. The nub of our weakness seems to be the compromise with principle that may be compelled in allowing the liberty to be different.

But time and history are on our side. Compelling uniformity is a confession, not of strength, but of weakness. The unity which would be uniformity is no aim which modern men who have had a taste of real democracy will ever accept.

When the war came, I began to learn something about administration and the function of an executive. I took the job of coördinating the Federal Government programs for soldier and war workers' recreation, for schools and health and sanitation and welfare services around camps and boom towns, partly because I knew I had had none of that experience and I wanted it. I wish I had had Barnard and Mayo and some of Mary Follett then. I had never heard of them. When that job was pretty well under control, I moved over to the State Department, whose work really became my great love. Once more, I had to find the effective expression of what I had learned after the job was done.

This is where the churches are weak; they just don't know the problems of the executive who has to make choices which involve ethical and moral considerations. Here is a simple example: The receptionist at our church is a very important person, for we have two thousand members and are in the center of the downtown area. She just could not do the job, as the rector and the vestry knew from long efforts to improve her work. After much heart searching it was decided that she must go. Now in an Episcopal Church the rector runs the show and does the hiring. That would seem to mean he should also do the firing. But the vestry knew the young woman and her mother would still be in the church, and it would be a little hard for the rector to go on as their pastor if he fired her—you know! So who do you think fired her? I did; and they still look at me a little cross-eyed when they come into church.

That was wrong. We should have made the rector fire her, in order to have some direct understanding of what laymen are up against. A similar problem is up with our new rector, and believe me, the vestry has learned its lesson. We have needled him, but we aren't doing the firing for him. I take real pleasure in making him uncomfortable, much as I love him, until he steels himself to do what he must do. His is an easier case, too, as a matter of fact; what if you have an employee, fifty-five years old, left in a position by prior buckpassers, absolutely incompetent in that place and messing up the whole organization, but with a wife and four fine children in school and college and no prospect of any other job? Do you wonder if that executive, who gets no help from the church in what keeps him awake nights, doesn't come often to the worship services?

DEMOCRACY IN POLITICS AND ECONOMICS

The experience in coördinating health, education, welfare, and recreation involved running a small nationwide organization of 350 or 400, but it also involved competition with another organization, the Federal Works Agency, which had money under the Lanham Act for schools, hospitals, health centers, sewers and water lines, and recreation centers. That introduced me to the frustration of the subordinate who just can't get his job done because of competition and interference up higher somewhere. Pay is one reason why government doesn't get or keep good men, but frustration is a good deal more important. When we thought we had the battle won, the WPA left overs in the Federal Works Agency ran to Harry Hopkins or Mrs. Roosevelt; or Allen Johnstone, their general counsel, ran to Jimmy Byrnes. The battle was lost. That kind of warfare continued when I went to the State Department, this time more successfully, with the remnants of the New Dealers in the Treasury, in the Department of Justice, and in the Foreign Economic Administration. After four years and a half of battling New Dealers, I was somewhat amused to hear that somebody had described me as a New Dealer.

The State Department with its worldwide operation in over three hundred regional offices presents a fascinating problem in administration which I hope Dean Acheson can begin to solve on the basis of the Hoover Commission report. Good administration in that first line of our peacetime defense is one of the most necessary of government operations. I am not very optimistic, because really good administrative ability is not universal, and in government at the top it is certainly rare.

Frustration as a subordinate executive, and then service as labor consultant for Monsanto led me into the study and contemplation of the literature of labor relations. All of which put me right in the middle of this problem of competition of values and of objectives in our modern American civilization, to say nothing of worldwide conflicts over the same questions. Are there any answers? Is there any way that our strong, intelligent young men who came out of educational institutions today can be prepared for the kind of secular world with all its moral problems in which they will take their part?

I suppose I have no business commenting on educational theory and the curriculum, but I get so annoyed at "school men" that in self-defense, perhaps, here goes. Elton Mayo is unduly critical, perhaps, when he describes sociology, psychology, and political science as the unsuccessful sciences, but I must say I think he has something when he says: "One cannot fail to be struck by the extent of the failure of the latter [the "unsuccessful" sciences] to communicate to students a skill that is directly useful in human situations." This may be unkind: "Sociology is highly developed but mainly as an exercise in the acquisition of scholarship. Students are taught to write books about each other's books."

An experiment worth watching and copying comes from the injection of a lawyer, who had gone into State and become director of public relations, into the position of President of Dartmouth. John Dickey has put in as a compulsory course for all seniors (six hundred of them) what he calls the Great Issues Course. They hear a weekly lecture by an outside layman, prefaced by an explanatory lecture by the related faculty man, on domestic politics and international relations, on the humanities and the sciences and the arts, and they end with a group of lectures on the moral and religious stock in trade of the minds of top-rank thinkers and citizens. The laboratory work meanwhile consists of a daily reading of the New York *Times* or *Herald Tribune;* plus in the first semester an essay on the news handling, during a brief seven-day period, of some four or five picked issues by a group of general newspapers and periodicals; plus in the second semester an essay on the handling of a similar set of issues by a set of regular publications by pressure groups in the broad sense, the Farm Bureau Federation, the CIO and A.F. of L., the Federal Council and National Catholic Welfare Conference, the NAM and U.S. Chamber of Commerce and American Management Association, the American Legion and VFW, the National Federation of Womens Clubs and the League of Women Voters.

That begins to meet Mr. Mayo's challenge. That is the stuff of real social understanding. It also produces some degree of violent and unfavorable reaction from some seniors. Yet is there any educated American who comes out of college that can afford to be ignorant of all the social pressures in the community, of all the situations where social skills are needed?

More than that, the effect of the course, interpreted in the light of the laboratory work, is to give some integration of the man's college work. Every department gets into it, and the leadership of the faculty committee that conducts it is annually rotated among the college's department heads. Where indeed is integration to come from? The Harvard study agrees it is essential and so does President Conant in his last book on *Education in a Divided World*. But their answers are pretty weak. When you look at the immense diversity of available courses in a modern high school, with no real effort anywhere that I know of to find the integration we need, one can't find much hope in the Harvard study's conclusion. Hear this: "Belief in the dignity and mutual obligation of man is the common ground between these contrasting but mutually necessary forces in our culture. . . . This belief is the fruit at once of religion, of the Western tradition, and of the American tradition." Does that "common ground" create any unity between the favored boy who is taking the "classical" course in high school that leads him to college, the boy who is studying pharmacy, the one heading for agriculture, and the boy who is taking the machine or electrical trades course? Not if I know anything about high schools. The Hi Y is doing a lot more integrating than that kind of pious language.

Religion is the only possible integrating factor for us, the religion of the Jewish-Christian tradition. The new generation is not getting it adequately now, at least in part because it is considering religion as an extracurricular activity. So there we are up against the problem of religion in the public schools. Is there any answer at all?

The first answer is of course far better teaching of religion in church school on Sunday. A second answer is certainly released-time education off the premises on weekdays, which I believe will be held constitutional as the Supreme Court catches up on its understanding of the problem. The Court does not know much about some basic religious problems, but it is open-minded, and does learn. It forced the flag salute on Jehovah's Witnesses, over the protesting argument of an American Bar Association Committee on the Bill of Rights of which I was a member, but in a few years we helped persuade a reversal.

A more important step is the inclusion in the ordinary curriculum of considerably more general study of religion in connection with all courses where it is relevant. That is recommended by a committee of the American Council on Education on which were included official representatives of Catholics, Jews, and Protestants. In a course on social studies why should not students in Houston high schools visit types of all churches in the community and have presented enough of their history and forms of worship to get some light on them as a part of the life of Houston as a community? It is surely as important as a visit to the ship channel or an oil refinery or a soap plant.

A private university should do more. It certainly should give official sanction not only as Rice does for these lectures, but as we do at Yale for the presence of a college chaplain, a Christian Association and Newman Club and Hillel Foundation, and the participation and coördination of the work of denominational pastors related to their members in the student body. Nothing is more important than the attitude and activity in religion of the president and trustees and faculty.

That leads me to one observation made as a member of

the Yale Alumni Council and chairman of its committee on religious life and study at Yale. There are various ideas about education these days, those of the conservatives headed by Hutchins, of the progressives, of the middle-of-the-road people (where I find myself, as in so many other issues). There are strong Christian theologians and dogmatic materialists. Those positions all raise the question as to what is and should be the integrating factor in education and life. Is it not the duty of a university, considered in its basic character as a group of thinking men gathered around a library, at whose feet students sit to learn from their discussions, to bring about a discussion, thoughtful and open-minded, a real conference process on this absolutely fundamental issue? At Yale we have the greatest of the interdenominational theological seminaries, and at first I thought it was its function to start this process, but it should stem from the center of the university, the president and corporation and all the faculty. Nevertheless the Divinity School ought to be near the center of the activity, for theology and the interpretation of its principles for a modern day are an essential part of securing a unity in our presently conflicting diversity. The effects of all that process if it once gets under way will surely show up in the next generation and perhaps sooner.

In the meantime what can be done for and by us laymen on the outside? The Federal Council of Churches and the World Council are effectively at work on it. At Amsterdam the committee on the laity in the church pointed out forcefully that the churches had left the laymen living in two separate worlds, in the satisfaction of a kind of religious experience on Sunday, and in a completely different and irrelevant complexity of secular problems on weekdays in spite of the necessity for loyalty to Christ to display itself in every phase of life. I have just received the outline of a worldwide study requested of all member churches of the World Council each in its own country, of the Bible and the Church's Message to the World, the Evangelization of Man in Modern Mass Society, and Christian Action in Society. The returns from that project in the five years to the next assembly will be most stimulating as it works through all denominations.

The Federal Council began two years ago to study how Christian principles can be applied in economic life. After the Pittsburgh Conference a new department was set up and a committee picked which is an extraordinarily effective and representative group. It has some few clergy, but mostly real lay men and women. It has six economists, the first time any national or denominational church group thought to join economists in studying economic problems. Our best employer representatives and labor spokesmen are not the big names (who are also on the committee) but people with a personnel management background and close-to-earth contact with collective bargaining. We have theologians as well as preachers. The important product of the first year and a half is liking and respect for each other, and a core of basic thinking and discussion.

Now the Rockefeller Foundation has given us $100,000 for a three-year study of how to apply religion in economic life. Our study committee has just decided that we want to examine, with a staff of a top-notch economist and a new minister who graduated first in economics and spent a number of years in business, what are the moral and ethical problems that trouble—or should trouble—Christian men and women who are active in what can be described generally as pressure groups, labor, business, veterans, farm, women, and perhaps a few others. We want especially to see how those people mix in churches, and what churches do for and to them to help make them responsible citizens of a larger community. They, like most of us, have merged a certain amount of their individual self-interest in the cause or enterprise where they and others work for a common purpose. But what if the purpose begins to conflict with the larger purpose of a larger group that includes them also, or with the competing purposes of another similar group? Can the church and religion help to solve this basic conflict of our democracy, which unresolved can tear us apart, and quite literally destroy our civilization? The atomic physicists who are so disturbed by their first contacts with political realities, the professors like Schumpeter who see a disintegrating capitalism in the face of irresistible revolutionary masses, the more reasonable religious thinkers like Canon Demant who see today signs that have in the past marked the decline of civilizations, do not disturb me much. Dealing with the strengthening of the religious sources of democracy, and the application of those and other Christian principles to our daily living and its pressure groups, that is the most pressing task in a still growing youthful world.

The Federal Council study will only contribute to any such effort as it stays close to people. When it is done, it will still not make the impact unless it is put in the language of the laymen. It will not reach the laymen unless each denomination takes the product and makes it its own by a conference process that relates it to its own people and its own tradition. To cities it may also come through the ministerial association or local council of churches.

This is a project that perhaps illustrates the modern application of the historical background from which I began, and uses all the complex system of organizations in which we live. We start with our ideal of equality which makes the problem of the frustrated little man in a big society just as important as the worries of the harassed executive. We look for the contribution of many and varied elements in the community. We insist on unity in that diversity and try to find it in loyalty to one God, and to a common Master.